DIVERSITY IN ACTION

Diversity in Medicine

CATHLEEN SMALL

rosen publishing's
rosen central

New York

Published in 2019 by The Rosen Publishing Group, Inc.
29 East 21st Street
New York, NY 10010

First Edition

Produced for Rosen by Calcium
Editors for Calcium: Sarah Eason and Jennifer Sanderson
Designer: Simon Borrough
Picture researcher: Rachel Blount

Photo credits: Cover photo of Kumar Bahuleyan: Indo American Hospital; Inside: Dr. Patricia Bath: pp. 14, 15; Indo American Hospital: p. 26; Dreamstime: Starstock: p. 8; Massachusetts General Hospital: p. 40; Shutterstock: Africa Studio: p. 12; ALPA PROD: pp. 1, 7; Valeriya Anufriyeva: p. 13; Olesia Bilkei: p. 35; CandyBox Images: p. 24; Chombosan: p. 6; Fri9thsep: p. 31; Image Point Fr: p. 39; Herbert Kratky: p. 9; Loveischiangrai: p. 23; Michaeljung: pp. 3, 5, 11; Monkey Business Images: pp. 18, 41; Michail Petrov: p. 37; Photographee.eu: p. 10; Phovoir: p. 36; Juri Pozzi: p. 28; Thanyawat Rachtiwa: p. 4; ShutterstockProfessional: p. 22; Jenny Sturm: p. 34; Travel Stock: p. 29; Tukaram.Karve: p. 27; Vetkit: p. 38; Vgstockstudio: pp. 42–43; Wavebreakmedia: pp. 16, 17; Dmytro Zinkevych: p. 19; The Cleveland Clinic: pp. 32, 33; Wikimedia Commons: Thomas R Machnitzki: p. 25; Wellcome Images: pp. 20, 21.

Cataloging-in-Publication Data

Names: Small, Cathleen.
Title: Diversity in medicine / Cathleen Small.
Description: New York : Rosen Central, 2019. | Series: Diversity in action | Includes glossary and index.
Identifiers: ISBN 9781499440829 (pbk.) | ISBN 9781499440836 (library bound)
Subjects: LCSH: Medicine—Juvenile literature. | Medical innovations—Juvenile literature. | Cultural pluralism—Juvenile literature.
Classification: LCC R130.5 S63 2019 | DDC 616.07—dc23

Manufactured in the United States of America

Contents

Diversity on the Rise

In the United States, the field of medicine used to be dominated by white male doctors and white female nurses. Over the past several decades, that has changed. The medical field now includes doctors, nurses, and other medical professionals from many different ethnicities and cultural backgrounds. There are numerous female doctors and male nurses.

Medicine in the Jim Crow South

It has been a long road to diversity in medicine, particularly where doctors are concerned. For example, in 1905, in the whole of Georgia, there were only sixty-five black doctors. While you might think these doctors would have busy medical practices among the black community, the opposite was true: many black people felt that white doctors were better educated than black ones, so they preferred to be seen by white doctors. White citizens did not go to black doctors either. This was the Jim Crow South, after all, where black people and white people were not allowed in the same restaurants.

The field of medicine includes doctors, nurses, therapists, physicians' assistants, lab technicians, and many more medical staff members.

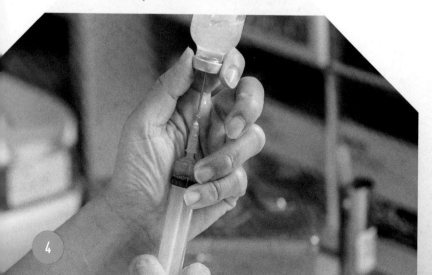

Racial Diversity in Medicine Today

Even today, according to the Bureau of Labor Statistics (BLS), just over 8 percent of practicing physicians in the United States are black. The percentage of Hispanic or Latinx physicians is even smaller, at just 6.8 percent. Asian physicians make up only 18 percent of the total number of physicians and surgeons in the United States. In the medical field as a whole, which includes chiropractors, dentists, physical therapists, paramedics, and more, 76.5 percent of practitioners and staff are white, while 11.9 percent are black, 9.4 percent are Asian, and 8.2 percent are Hispanic or Latinx.

International Medical Graduates

International medical graduates—people who earned their medical degree outside of the United States—make up 32 percent of the physician workforce in the United States. Nearly half of that segment of the workforce is made up of physicians who earned their degrees in lower-income countries, including developing nations. Physicians trained in lower-income countries make up 29 percent of physicians in West Virginia, 27 percent in New Jersey, and 26 percent in Michigan. Montana, Idaho, and Alaska all had the lowest numbers of these physicians practicing, with doctors from low-income countries making up fewer than 2 percent of the practicing physicians in each of those states.

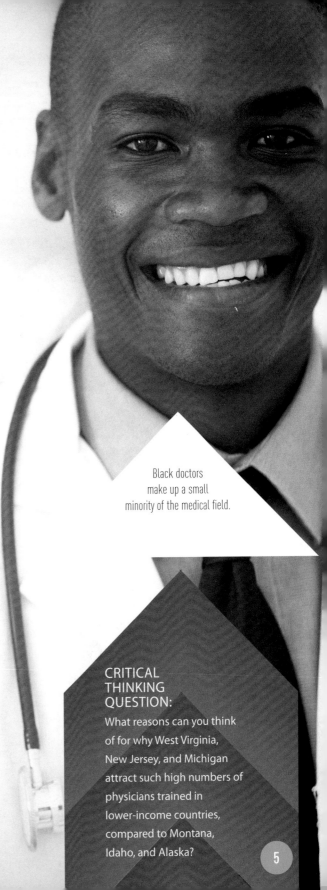

Black doctors make up a small minority of the medical field.

CRITICAL THINKING QUESTION:
What reasons can you think of for why West Virginia, New Jersey, and Michigan attract such high numbers of physicians trained in lower-income countries, compared to Montana, Idaho, and Alaska?

Gender Diversity in Medicine

The numbers are skewed by gender, too. In the medical field, 75 percent of practitioners and staff are women. But looking at just doctors, only 40 percent are women. Conversely, 89.9 percent of registered nurses are women and female speech therapists make up an eye-opening 98 percent of that field. These statistics show that while the gender demographic of physicians has become more diverse, with women making up almost half of physicians, the gender split in nurses is still very much unequal, with very few male nurses compared to female.

The Importance of Diversity in Medicine

Diversity in the medical field is important because it ensures better health, lower healthcare costs, and less difference in quality of healthcare. Different ethnic groups, for example, face different health challenges, and having a medical team knowledgeable of and sensitive to these challenges ensures better treatment.

Although the majority of nurses are women, the number of female doctors is much smaller.

CRITICAL THINKING QUESTION:
The percentages of male occupational therapists and physical therapists are very low, too. Why do you suppose there are so few male nurses and therapists?

Patients also tend to be more comfortable with medical staff they can relate to. This means that they are more likely to go to the doctor when they need to and not ignore potentially dangerous signs of illness. A black doctor who went to medical school in the 1970s, when few black men were becoming doctors in the United States, told the story of an older black woman entering a hospital that had very old-fashioned practices. This was in the South in the 1970s, when racism was common, even though blatant racist practices had long been against the law. The young doctor's heart hurt as he saw how embarrassed the older woman was at the care she received, which was medically appropriate but did not take into account cultural sensitivity and the woman's dignity. A black doctor, the young man felt, would better understand how to offer the woman care without making her feel like a vulnerable, second-class citizen.

Physical, occupational, and speech therapists also make up a significant portion of the medical field.

Many institutions of higher learning have recognized the lack of diversity in certain segments of the healthcare industry and are actively working to change it. Medical schools are trying to attract more diverse populations of students, and medical practices are trying to include more diversity among their physicians. Hopefully, this trend toward diversifying the medical field will continue as the twenty-first century progresses.

Bennet Omalu:

Discovering Chronic Traumatic Encephalopathy

American football is a sport loved by millions and the Super Bowl is one of the most popular televised sporting events. Football, however, has a darker side, too: chronic traumatic encephalopathy (CTE). CTE is a player injury that results in serious difficulty and even death for players who experience it. Although CTE gained attention as the result of a distinctly American sport, the physician who discovered it and published important findings of it was not born in the United States.

From Nigeria to the United States

Bennet Omalu was born in southeastern Nigeria. Though he and his six siblings had to flee their home during the Nigerian Civil War in the late 1960s, they were able to return to it after a couple of years, and Omalu had a reasonably typical upbringing. His mother was a seamstress and his father was a community leader and a civil engineer. Omalu began medical school at the University of Nigeria when he was sixteen years old. He graduated with his medical degree in 1990. Four years later, disappointed with the political system in Nigeria, Omalu went to the United States to participate in an epidemiology fellowship at the University of Washington in Seattle. He then moved to New York City and did a residency program for anatomic and clinical pathology.

Omalu's next step was to train as a forensic pathologist at the coroner's office in Pittsburgh, Pennsylvania. There, he developed an interest in neuropathology, which led to his work on CTE.

Omalu married Prema Mutiso, a Kenyan nurse. Together they have two children.

Omalu performed an autopsy on a Pittsburgh Steelers football player, Mike Webster. Omalu was suspicious that Webster's death was a result of chronic concussions suffered during his time as a professional football player, so he studied Webster's brain. Although the brain looked normal, Omalu did independent studies of the brain tissue (which he paid for himself) and learned that a specific protein was found in Webster's brain tissue that supported Omalu's suspicions.

Omalu's Findings

In 2005, Omalu published a report of his findings and suggested that further study was needed to see whether CTE was present in other deceased football players. While the National Football League (NFL) initially dismissed Omalu's findings, Omalu found the same protein in the brains of four other deceased NFL players. It took nearly seven years, but eventually the NFL recognized the significance of Omalu's findings and began to take steps to try to prevent CTE.

NOT JUST FOOTBALL

Wrestlers, boxers, hockey players, rugby players, and soccer players have also been found to have CTE. So too have victims of domestic violence and military personnel. CTE is a difficult disease because the symptoms often do not begin to appear until well after the head injuries occur.

9

Racial Diversity in Medicine

While racial diversity in the medical field has increased in recent decades, medicine is still very much a field dominated by white people. In a way, this is not surprising, since the makeup of the United States as a whole is mostly white. Based on census data from 2016, people who identified only as white made up 61.3 percent of the US population. The largest minority group in the United States was Hispanic/Latinx, making up 12.8 percent of the population. Black people were the second largest minority group, making up 12.3 percent of the population. Asians made up 5.7 percent of the population. The rest of the population is made up of Native Americans and Native Hawaiian/Pacific Islanders. So in a way, it stands to reason that white people would make up the largest group of the medical workforce.

The medical field as a whole is mostly staffed by white people.

Although black people make up more than 12 percent of the population of the United States, they make up only 8 percent of US physicians.

Breakdown of Racial Diversity

Statistics show that the medical field is made up of 76.5 white people, roughly 12 percent black, approximately 9 percent Asian, and around 8 percent Hispanic/Latinx. The percentages total more than one hundred because some people identify as both white and another race, such as white and Latinx. These numbers are not far from an accurate representation of the population spread of the United States, but the numbers change in specific fields within medicine. For example, among physicians, 72 percent are white, roughly 8 percent are black, roughly 7 percent are Hispanic/Latinx, and roughly 18 percent are Asian.

When we move into something like speech-language pathologists, the percentages are drastically different from the general population breakdown. White people make up 93 percent of that field, with black practitioners making up nearly 3 percent, Asians making up nearly 3 percent, and Hispanic/Latinx making up 10 percent. This is significant because speech-language pathologists work with children and adults who have speech difficulties. They also work with those for whom English is a new language and those who may speak slightly different dialects. Working with a speech provider who is familiar with the specific language patterns they are used to, would be of great benefit.

CRITICAL THINKING QUESTION:

Can you think of reasons that might explain the disproportionate percentages of minorities working in the medical field?

Benefits to Racial Diversity in Medicine

There are other benefits of having a more racially diverse workforce in medicine. Minorities have significantly worse health indicators than white people in the United States. Health indicators are characteristics of a given population that can be measured to indicate the overall health of that particular population group. These can be death rate, life expectancy, infant mortality, obesity, diabetes, cancer incidence, high blood pressure, smoking habits, exercise habits, and more. According to the Stanford University Minority Medical Alliance (SUMMA), in the United States, black people, Puerto Ricans, Mexicans, and Native Americans generally have lower life expectancy, more chronic disease, and poorer pregnancy outcomes than white citizens. They also obtain preventative healthcare services and certain medical procedures less often than white citizens.

CRITICAL THINKING QUESTION:
What reasons can you think of to explain why health indicators are worse in minority populations?

Increasing diversity in the medical field can help combat these poor statistics. Minority doctors are more likely than white doctors to practice in underserved areas of the country, where many of the people from minority groups live.

Health indicators in the black community are lower than in the white community.

They are also more likely to provide care for minorities and poor, uninsured, or underinsured people, who might not otherwise receive care. Minority patients often feel a sense of affinity with medical professionals who are the same race as them. The patients are more likely to be open and honest about their health with physicians they can relate to, which leads to better care for them.

Racial diversity in medicine leads to better learning and better cultural competency for all in the field. If the group of medical professionals discussing important medical issues is all one race, the conversation will be limited—people from one race typically have similar experiences and views on a large scale, though their personal beliefs undoubtedly differ here and there. But when a diverse group of people discuss the same issues, they bring their different backgrounds and ideas to the conversation. For example, there are certain diseases and conditions that affect certain populations more frequently. One such condition is sickle-cell disease. It affects mostly black children, with some Hispanic or Middle Eastern children also affected. Physicians working with mostly white children will have a basic knowledge of sickle-cell disease from medical school, but they may not be knowledgeable on the latest research because it is not a disease that typically affects their patients. In a case like this, the experience of physicians serving the black, Hispanic/Latinx, and Middle Eastern populations would be hugely important.

Medical specialists from a particular racial group have unique insights into medical issues facing the people in that racial group.

Patricia Bath:

Revolutionizing Ophthalmology

Entering the field of medicine, Patricia Bath faced multiple challenges. She was a woman trying to enter a male-dominated field and she was black in a predominantly white field. She was also poor in a field that is typically dominated by upper-middle-class or upper-class people. However, that did not stop her from becoming an important contributor to the field of medicine. She moved beyond every obstacle in her path.

Academic Ambition

Bath was born during World War II in Harlem, New York. Her father, Rupert Bath, was an immigrant from Trinidad who broke barriers of his own: He was the New York City subway's first black motorman. Her mother, Gladys, was a homemaker and a housekeeper who was descended from slaves. While Bath's parents came from modest backgrounds and had modest means, they encouraged Bath's academic ambitions. Bath was recognized as a bright, promising student and loved math and science. She graduated high school in fewer than three years. During her time in high school, Bath won a National Science Foundation (NSF)

Patricia Bath revolutionized treatment for cataracts—an eye problem prevalent in elderly people but also present in some younger people.

scholarship and contributed to an important study on the connection between nutrition, stress, and cancer. These accolades helped her earn a place in college and medical school.

After graduating, Bath began to study children's health, and she discovered that there was a disproportionate rate of blindness in racial minorities and poor people. She began to dedicate herself to providing eye care to populations that had been underserved up to that point. She ultimately became the first black woman to do a residency in ophthalmology at New York University, and in 1978, she cofounded the American Institute for the Prevention of Blindness.

Sight-Saving Inventions

In her work in ophthalmology, Bath invented several important devices that revolutionized the field. The first was the Laserphaco Probe, a laser device that greatly improved cataract treatment. She obtained a patent for the device in 1988, becoming the first black woman to gain a patent for a medical device. The Laserphaco Probe (which has since been refined) is still used internationally to treat cataracts today. Bath patented two other devices related to the device, as well as earning one patent for an ultrasound method she developed to treat cataracts.

It is estimated that millions of people around the world have had their sight restored thanks to Bath's inventions.

WHAT ARE CATARACTS?
Cataracts are a condition that cloud the lens of the eye, which is normally clear. They are slow to develop, but eventually those suffering from cataracts feel as if they are looking through cloudy, fogged-up glasses. Left long enough, cataracts can cause blindness. Cataracts typically worsen as people age, but some conditions can cause cataracts or speed their development, including diabetes and some genetic conditions.

15

Gender Diversity in Medicine

Taking into account all of the jobs in healthcare and related industries, the 2017 data from the BLS shows that 75 percent of all people working in the healthcare field are women.

Gender Breakdown in Medicine

That number is slightly misleading, though. Certain areas have a very high percentage of women, which brings up the average percentage across other jobs. For example, 94 percent of dieticians and nutritionists are female, and nearly 90 percent of registered nurses are female. However, only 35.8 percent of dentists are women.

Looking at doctors and surgeons, which used to be male-dominated careers, the numbers are surprisingly even. The first licensed female doctor in the United States, Elizabeth Blackwell, graduated from medical school in 1849.

The numbers of men and women in medicine vary widely depending on which specific medical profession you look at.

CRITICAL
THINKING
QUESTION:
Why do you think female
doctors tend to work in fields
like pediatrics and obstetrics,
instead of surgery? What
about these fields do you think
attracts women versus men?

As of 2017 data, 40 percent of physicians and surgeons are women. That percentage changes when the specific types of specialties are broken down. For example, surgeons tend to be mainly male, but pediatricians, family doctors, and obstetricians tend to be mostly female.

The numbers are continuing to trend toward more women in the medical field. According to the Association of American Medical Colleges (AAMC), in 2016 the number of women enrolling in medical school reached a ten-year high. AAMC also found that the breakdown of men and women enrolling was almost an even split, with 49.8 percent of enrollees being women and 50.2 percent being men.

Importance of Gender Diversity

Gender diversity is important in the medical field for a number of reasons. Many people are most comfortable seeing a doctor of their same gender. The more comfortable a patient is, the better healthcare he or she will receive.

In the United States, most pediatricians are women, as are most family doctors.

Medicine involves a lot of collaborative research and consultation. A 2010 study of 699 participants showed that in science, teams with members from both genders performed the best in a variety of tasks. The study showed that women tend to be more socially perceptive (understanding how people think and feel), which resulted in teams with women on them having greater participation. A similar study of five hundred scientists and engineers showed that women tended to be stronger at recognizing the expertise of other team members, which resulted in a more collaborative team effort.

The study also found that women tended to place more emphasis on educational experience when determining expertise, whereas men tended to place more value on things like gender itself. All-female teams, however, were no more effective overall than all-male teams, indicating that a mix of genders was better for teamwork than teams of all one gender.

Gender diversity is also important because men and women tend to look at problems differently. Medicine is a complicated field, and sometimes illnesses and conditions are difficult to diagnose or treat. Sometimes having a fresh viewpoint can help pinpoint a cause or determine a plan of treatment. That is why some people go for second opinions to ensure the first doctor's diagnosis and treatment plan were satisfactory. When a person gets a second opinion, it is not necessarily from a doctor of the opposite gender. However, the idea is the same: a different set of eyes, a different perspective, or a different background might provide much-needed insight. There are many medical conditions that have some basis in gender, so having medical professionals of both genders can help ensure that a person very familiar with a medical condition specific to a gender is available to consult if necessary.

Often people feel most comfortable seeing a doctor who is the same gender as they are.

CRITICAL THINKING QUESTION:
Besides childbirth, what other areas of healthcare can you think of that might benefit from having a practitioner of a specific gender available?

For example, while male physicians are perfectly capable of delivering babies, women have a first-person understanding of how the female body works and, if they have had a baby themselves, what childbirth entails. That perspective can be important.

The Field Dominated by Women

Gender diversity is surprisingly strong in medicine, given that the field started out with stereotypes of all doctors being male and all nurses being female. Nursing is still a very female-dominated field, but it is slowly attracting more men. According to the United States Census Bureau, in 1970, male registered nurses made up only 2.7 percent of the field. As of 2011, that number had increased to 9.6 percent.

If only other types of diversity were as well represented in medicine, the field could be a model for diversity. However, certain other groups are drastically underrepresented in the field, which means medicine still has a long way to go before it is truly diverse.

Obstetrics is another segment of the medical field dominated by women.

19

Elizabeth Blackwell:

The First US Female Doctor

Change has to start with someone, and when it comes to women becoming doctors, that someone was Elizabeth Blackwell. Blackwell became the first woman in the United States to earn an M.D. degree.

Blackwell was not born in the United States—she was born in England in 1821. As a result of her parents' interest in helping abolish slavery, her family moved to the United States in 1832. Blackwell and her siblings learned from their parents' activism and ultimately ended up supporting the anti-slavery movement and the women's rights movement themselves as adults.

Even as a young woman, Elizabeth Blackwell, shown here, was determined to graduate from medical school and become a doctor.

A Life-Changing Conversation

Blackwell did not always envision herself becoming a doctor. In fact, at school she hated studying medical and life sciences, and she preferred studying history and metaphysics. After she finished school, she became a teacher. Later, when a close friend who was dying shared that she felt she would have suffered far less if her doctor had been a woman, Blackwell was inspired to change careers. It was not an easy change, though. Most medical schools would not consider allowing a woman to study.

Geneva Medical College in western New York, however, agreed to let her apply but let the student body (which was all male) vote on whether she would be accepted. Some of the male students voted yes as a joke, but it was enough to earn Blackwell her spot among them.

In 1849, Blackwell graduated as the first woman in the United States to become a doctor of medicine. She originally aspired to be a surgeon and worked for a couple of years in London, England, and Paris, France, but in 1851 she returned to the United States after losing her sight in one eye.

Not a Warm Welcome

Blackwell was not welcomed into the medical community with open arms. In fact, she found many patients would not see her because she was a woman, and many male doctors were not willing to work with her. After running into several dead ends for jobs, she opened her own practice in a rented room where she saw patients three days a week. By 1857, that single-room clinic had become the New York Infirmary for Women and Children. Blackwell worked with her sister Dr. Emily Blackwell and Dr. Marie Zakrzewska. A decade later, the infirmary opened a medical college for women and was dedicated to providing medical care for the poor. Blackwell practiced medicine for one-quarter of a century before retiring due to ill health.

HOSPITALS FOR WOMEN

While most medical facilities see both men and women, there are some that specialize in the care of female patients. For example, in 1857 Elizabeth Blackwell established the New York Infirmary for Women and Children. In the 1870s, the New Hospital for Women was opened in London, England. It catered to poor women who could not afford to access quality medical care. Female practitioners staffed the hospital. It was renamed the Elizabeth Garrett Anderson Hospital in 1918, after one of the first British female physicians.

Economic and Social Diversity in Medicine

It is incredibly expensive to prepare to work in the medical field. Most positions in the field require some sort of post–high school education.

The Cost of Entering Medicine

Depending on the career choice in the field, that post–high school education can be incredibly long and expensive. For example, there are different types of nurse, but to become a registered nurse, applicants need a bachelor's degree. According to a recent survey by the College Board, four years at an in-state public college will cost students a little more than $100,000. Four years at a private college will double that to more than $200,000 for four years. Becoming a doctor requires an additional four years of medical school, on top of the four-year bachelor's degree, and medical school ranges from approximately $200,000 to $300,000 for the four-year program, according to the AAMC.

CRITICAL THINKING QUESTION:

Why do you think colleges and medical schools do not attract more students with grants and scholarships? Can you think of reasons why students who need financial assistance might not receive it?

As it is so expensive to earn a degree to qualify for a position in the medical field, many people who join the field are from affluent backgrounds. That is particularly true for aspiring doctors. According to the AAMC, most medical students have parents with advanced degrees. The AAMC also found that in the past several decades, roughly 50 percent of students in medical schools have come from families who are in the top 25 percent of the US population in terms of income. On average, these families earned more than twice as much per year as the median family income in the United States. In other words, the majority of medical students in the United States come from relatively wealthy families.

Importance of Socioeconomic Diversity in Medicine

One reason why it is important to have a socially and economically diverse workforce in medicine is that it accurately represents the makeup of the United States. There are many wealthy parts of the United States, but there are also many poorer and poverty-stricken places. These poor and impoverished areas are the ones that often lack adequate medical care, which creates a vicious cycle: Economically disadvantaged people need to be able to work to support themselves and their families. If they are sick and cannot get adequate medical care, then they cannot work. And the cycle of poverty and illness continues.

Some doctors do relief work in poor communities. Most often, those doctors are people who have ties to poorer communities.

Diversity in Medicine

When medical schools recruit students from disadvantaged and impoverished areas, some of the students will graduate and choose to work in or near where they grew up. They know firsthand how poor the medical care is, and many of them want to give back by improving healthcare in their hometowns.

When poor people receive care in facilities staffed with wealthier people, sometimes they have a difficult time trusting their care providers. When a wealthy doctor comes in to talk to a patient who perhaps never got past an elementary-school education, it can be difficult for the doctor to establish a relationship where the patient feels truly comfortable. And when health is at stake, it is important for people to feel comfortable with those treating them.

CRITICAL THINKING QUESTION: How do you think medical professionals from privileged backgrounds could work to make patients from less-privileged backgrounds feel more comfortable?

Obtaining a medical degree is expensive, but some medical schools recruit students from impoverished areas, too.

The town of Tutwiler has benefited from the service of osteopath Sister Anne Brooks for more than thirty years.

Bringing Quality Healthcare to the Poor

The Tutwiler Clinic in Tutwiler, Mississippi is one example of how medical professionals from poorer areas can make a difference. Tutwiler is an impoverished town of 3,500 residents, where many residents earn very little. For more than thirty years, an elderly osteopath named Sister Anne Brooks has cared for roughly 8,500 patients a year.

Sister Anne is familiar with poverty. She grew up in a Catholic boarding school after being abandoned by her father and her alcoholic mother. She spent seventeen years in a wheelchair before finally getting a correct diagnosis that allowed her to return to health. As a result of her own background, Sister Anne chose to practice in Tutwiler, where she has made an immense difference in her patients' lives. Opening her practice in 1983, Sister Anne learned the specific illnesses that her poverty-stricken patients tend to suffer from—for example, many catch impetigo as their homes do not having indoor plumbing—and she treated them accordingly. From the beginning, she has taught her patients how to eat healthier and live healthier, resulting in an overall improvement in the residents' well-being. And the residents of Tutwiler, in turn, have embraced Sister Anne and her clinic.

The hope is that if more economically diverse students began entering medical school, there would be more people like Sister Anne, who find a calling to provide care for the people who most often do not get it.

Kumar Bahuleyan:

A Great Doctor from Humble Origins

It may be difficult for poor people to work as doctors, but Kumar Bahuleyan is proof that it is not impossible.

From Poor Beginnings

Bahuleyan was born in Chemmanakary, a very poor village in Southern India. The village had no sanitation system, no water supply, no roads, no schools, and no electricity. Three of Bahuleyan's siblings died before the age of eight from a roundworm (a kind of parasite) infestation. Bahuleyan himself contracted smallpox, typhoid fever, and other childhood illnesses that are preventable or treatable in developed countries, but that were neither preventable nor treatable in his village.

Bahuleyan's father, recognizing his son's intelligence, was able to get him into a nearby school for the lower classes, even though the family could not afford to pay for tuition. Bahuleyan studied hard and excelled in that school and in the high school he attended. He was able to attend medical college, where he was a brilliant student. He did so well at medical college that the Indian government sent him to Scotland to study neurosurgery.

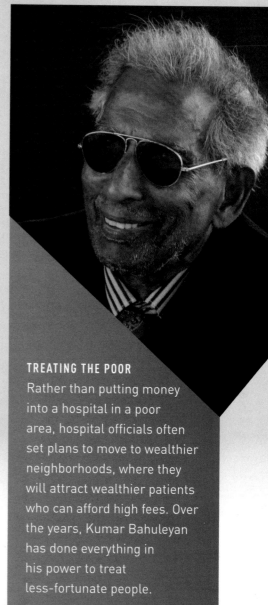

TREATING THE POOR
Rather than putting money into a hospital in a poor area, hospital officials often set plans to move to wealthier neighborhoods, where they will attract wealthier patients who can afford high fees. Over the years, Kumar Bahuleyan has done everything in his power to treat less-fortunate people.

However, after he obtained that education, Bahuleyan found that there were no jobs available in neurosurgery near his home. Poverty was so extreme that even basic medical care was hard to come by—there was really no need for neurosurgery.

To the United States and Back Again

This prompted Bahuleyan to move to Canada and then New York, where he attended Albany Medical College and settled in Buffalo, in western New York, to practice neurosurgery. When he returned to his village fifty years later, Bahuleyan discovered that essentially nothing had changed. It was still an extremely underdeveloped village, wracked by poverty. He decided to use the fortune he had made in Buffalo to improve the conditions in Chemmanakary. He built septic tanks so the village would have a sanitation system. He put in roads and built housing units. He also built a 200-bed hospital and set up clinics. Together, the hospital and clinics provide primary care and preventive care for children, as well as women's health. To ensure that the hospital would be staffed, he also plans to set up nursing and medical technician training institutes.

The lack of clean water and nutritious food can further complicate health issues in impoverished areas.

Bahuleyan is a shining example of a doctor who came from the poorest of poor villages but has done much to give back to it.

Chapter 5

Cultural Diversity in Medicine

The terms "race," "ethnicity," and "culture" are sometimes used interchangeably, but there are slight differences between them.

Defining Culture in Medicine

Race refers to major divisions among people, usually marked by physical differences—for example, skin color or eye shape. Ethnicity refers to a group that has a common national or cultural tradition. So while a person might be a member of the black race, he or she might be a black person born and raised in the United States or his or her ethnicity might be African.

Culture refers to the customs, arts, and social institutions of people from a particular region or social group. So, going back to the example of black Americans, their dominant culture may be that of black America, or if they emigrated from Africa, they may consider their dominant culture African, not American.

In medicine, this distinction is important because it affects how patients should be treated. There are certain diseases commonly associated with specific races, such as sickle-cell anemia occurring mostly in black people, and medical professionals need to be aware of them. When it comes to culture, medical personnel also have to be aware of cultural concerns and practice cultural sensitivity and cultural competence.

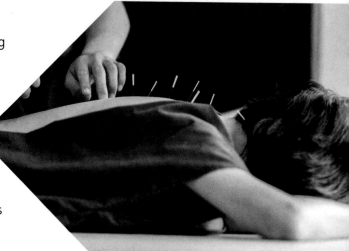

Acupuncture is just one type of eastern medicine.

CRITICAL
THINKING
QUESTION:
What other cultures can you
think of that are represented
in the United States?

Cultural Competence

Cultural competence means
being able to interact with
people from other cultures
and being respectful and
responsive to their beliefs
and practices regarding health.
It also refers to understanding the
cultural and linguistic needs of people
from other cultures. Different cultures
have different beliefs about healthcare and
treatment. While doctors are trained to do
whatever it takes to save the life of a patient,
the patient's wishes must be respected.

Eastern and Western Medicine

Not all cultures practice western medicine, which is the main
type of medicine practiced in the United States. Western
medicine has healthcare providers who treat diseases and
symptoms using drugs, surgery, or radiation. Many cultures
outside of the United States use eastern medicine. Eastern
medicine is based on beliefs formed thousands of years
ago. It is a holistic approach to medicine, which focuses on
treating the whole person. It relies on herbal medicines
and mind-body practices including acupuncture, tai chi,
and qi gong to treat health problems. More people
in the United States use eastern medicine along
with western medicine to manage their health,
but patients from other countries may
still prefer eastern medicine, and that
is something a culturally sensitive
medical provider needs to respect.

Although
the United States
is dominated by western
medicine, some cultures rely heavily
on eastern medical practices.

Respecting Patients' Beliefs

It may be hard for medical providers without a strong cultural competence to accept that their patients prefer eastern medicine to treat their illnesses. Doctors trained in western medicine tend to be very science- and data-driven. They are used to working with medicines that have been put through clinical trials to determine their effectiveness and safety. So it may be difficult for a doctor trained and practicing in this mindset to accept that a patient might turn down chemotherapy or another treatment used in western medicine in favor of the mind-body approach of eastern medicine.

It is important that a doctor try to understand a patient's wishes, though. Even if the doctor strongly believes western medicine is the best approach to treatment, another factor of medical care is establishing a bond with the patient. If the patient does not feel comfortable with a doctor because he or she knows the doctor does not subscribe to the patient's beliefs about healthcare, it will not be a positive relationship. The Health Professionals for Diversity Coalition suggests that culturally diversifying medicine can help medical professionals become more culturally competent. If medical professionals are exposed to a more diverse set of patients, they can become better versed in and more comfortable with other cultures. Similarly, if medical teams consist of people from different cultures, healthcare professionals can teach their colleagues how to respect the various cultures represented in the patients they see.

Cultural competence results in more satisfied patients who will hopefully feel comfortable coming to see their physician when problems arise. Cultural competence is also a win for the healthcare practice, according to Heka Healthcare Consulting. The president of Heka has said that healthcare facilities should operate like businesses in that they want to encourage repeat customers. In this case, the customers are the patients.

CRITICAL THINKING QUESTION:

What are some other ways you can think of to increase cultural competence in the medical field?

Medical care can be scary, and patients usually feel most comfortable with medical professionals whom they know will respect their beliefs.

If they feel their culture is respected and their concerns are heard, they are more likely to continue with that healthcare facility, which means the facility will be able to stay in business. In that sense, cultural competence is a win-win situation for both patients and healthcare professionals.

Maria Siemionow:

Groundbreaking Surgeon

Maria Siemionow was born in 1950 in Poland. At that time, her country was under the communist rule of the Soviet Union. It was a time when the government controlled everything and the country was economically devastated. It was difficult for citizens to rebuild after World War II because the Soviet government did not invest much money in the Polish economy.

Studying in Poland

Siemionow's parents were economists so her family did not struggle as much as many others, who relied on agriculture for their living. Siemionow earned her medical degree from Poznan Medical Academy in Poland and did her residency in orthopedics at the same institution, although it was difficult for women to get into medical school in Poland at the time.

A MAN'S WORLD

Orthopedic surgeons and orthopedists handle conditions of the muscular and skeletal systems. This medical field is heavily dominated by men. Recent estimates put the number of female orthopedic surgery residents at about 10 percent; the rest are men.

After medical school, Siemionow moved to the United States and earned a doctorate in microsurgery (using speciallialized microscopes and instruments to carry out intricate surgery) from the Christine Kleinert Institute for Hand and Micro Surgery in Louisville, Kentucky. She also did a hand surgery fellowship there.

Siemionow went on to become the director of plastic surgery research and the head of microsurgical training at the Cleveland Clinic Department of Plastic Surgery. While there, in 2008, she became famous by leading an eight-surgeon team through the first near-total face transplant in the world. The surgery took twenty-two hours, and the patient was a woman whose face had been disfigured by a shotgun blast fired at close range. More than 80 percent of the woman's face had to be transplanted, including her skin, muscles, eyelids, lips, and nose.

A Professor of Orthopedic Surgery

In 2014, Siemionow took a position at the University of Illinois at Chicago College of Medicine as a professor of orthopedic surgery. She specializes in the field of reconstructive transplantation, which involves performing surgeries such as hand and face transplants. She continues to expand her knowledge, working on hand and nerve surgery in transplantation, as well as reducing tissue rejection, which can be common in transplant surgery. Some of her research includes trying to fuse tissue-donor cells with recipient cells so that the recipient's body is less likely to reject the new transplanted tissues.

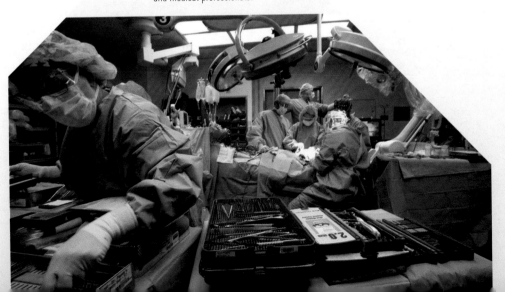

Transplant surgeries can be incredibly complicated and require a team of skilled doctors and medical professionals.

Diverse Abilities in Medicine

The United States is made up of many different groups of people. People may belong to more than one group. For example, one might identify as a woman, as Asian, as transgender, and as a new-language learner. Any person can undoubtedly identify many, many groups to which he or she belongs, with the main group being the human race.

Some of these groups are better represented than others in the United States. For example, women as a group are very well represented, given that as of the 2010 Census, women made up 50.8 percent of the US population. Black and Hispanic people make up a much smaller but still reasonably well represented group in the United States, at least in terms of numbers; members of each of these groups make up just over 12 percent of the US population.

Marginalized Populations

One group that is relatively large in number but that is consistently underrepresented is people with disabilities. According to the 2010 Census, approximately 19 percent of the US population has a disability.

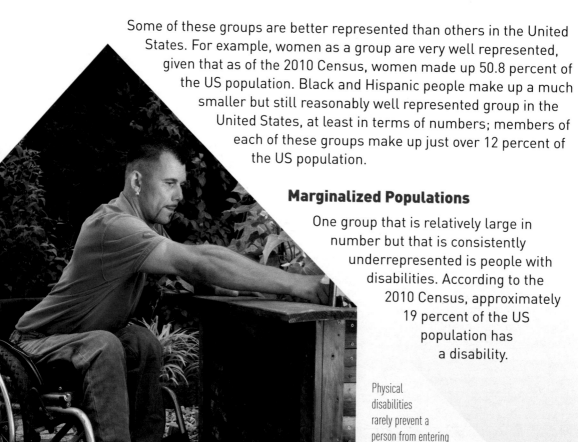

Physical disabilities rarely prevent a person from entering the medical field.

These disabilities range from relatively mild disabilities, such as difficulty lifting heavy objects or walking up stairs, to severe disabilities that significantly affect their lives. Some of these people were born with disabilities, and others became disabled later in life, due to either illness or injury. Although this is a significant proportion of the US population, this group tends to be consistently underrepresented when it comes to employment, education, and healthcare.

Number of Healthcare Providers with Disabilities

Much like the racial breakdown of people working in the medical field does not match up with the racial breakdown of people living in the United States, though 19 percent of Americans have some type of disability, the number of people with disabilities working in healthcare does not reflect that percentage. Although hard data on the number of medical practitioners with disabilities is difficult to find, estimates suggest that the number of doctors with disabilities is about 1 percent. There is evidence showing that in medical schools, people with disabilities make up only 0.3 to 2.7 percent of students, which leads to the logical conclusion that a very small percentage of graduating medical school students have disabilities.

It is not common to find a person with an intellectual disability working in the medical field.

The fact that there are so few medical practitioners with disabilities is problematic because patients tend to respond best to healthcare providers with whom they can identify. If a person with a disability is treated in a hospital where nearly everyone is fully-abled, the patient may not feel very comfortable—and comfort with the team is necessary for the patient to receive the best possible care.

For patients with disabilities, there is a vicious cycle: Being disabled means people are less likely to get good jobs and thus are more likely to be poor. If they are poor, they may be unable to access proper healthcare, which then leads to a situation where their health may suffer. People with disabilities recognize this cycle, because they have lived it all their lives. So diversifying the healthcare field to include more doctors and caregivers with disabilities would provide a better perspective into the unique healthcare challenges faced by people with disabilities.

Recognizing Unique Medical Challenges

People with disabilities can face unique medical challenges that a practitioner without much experience in disability may overlook.

Training in different disabilities can help medical providers understand the unique situations their patients with disabilities face.

For example, children with Down syndrome have a 50 percent chance of being born with a heart defect, an increased risk of developing leukemia, and an extremely high likelihood of developing hypothyroidism. A doctor treating Down syndrome needs to always be aware of these conditions. However, if that doctor has not been exposed to Down syndrome, he or she will be unlikely to have all of those in mind.

Laws and Barriers

Increasing diversity in the medical field is difficult for those with disabilities because there are certain barriers in place. The Americans with Disabilities Act (ADA), passed in 1990, guarantees equal opportunity for people with disabilities. And the Individuals with Disabilities Education Act (IDEA), also passed in 1990, guarantees people with disabilities the right to an education. However, neither of those two laws can govern the entrance requirements for medical school.

Medical schools typically have five technical standards students must meet, as designated by the AAMC: observation, communication, motor function, conceptual and quantitative analysis, and social skills. Meeting all of these may be challenging for people with disabilities. For example, a person with a physical disability might meet most of the standards but be unable to meet the motor function standard, leaving them ineligible for medical school.

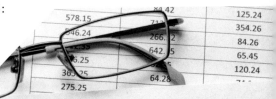

The ADA was landmark legislation that allowed people with disabilities far more access to education and careers than had been possible in the past.

While in school, students are eligible to receive supports and services to help them access the curriculum, but that is not necessarily true in medical school. The school can argue that the supports and services are too much of a modification to the curriculum, and patient safety might ultimately be compromised if the individual were allowed to continue in the program. Whether it is true that a patient's safety could be compromised is something no one can really prove: It is the school's word against that of the person with the disability.

Technology and the Future of People with Disabilities in Medicine

However, advances in technology are making medical school more accessible for some. For example, devices have been developed to help blind students read patient histories and electrocardiograms. Devices that can transcribe speech to help deaf students communicate in the operating room during their surgical and anesthesiology rotations.

Some schools are also starting to rethink their policies on admitting students with disabilities based on the technical standards. Some are even starting to rewrite the standards, which were first issued in 1979, to reflect the advances in technology that have made a career in medicine a more possible reality.

New technologies are making it easier for people with disabilities to enter the medical profession.

CRITICAL THINKING QUESTION:

If you were an inventor, what sort of technology would you invent to help people with disabilities working in the medical field?

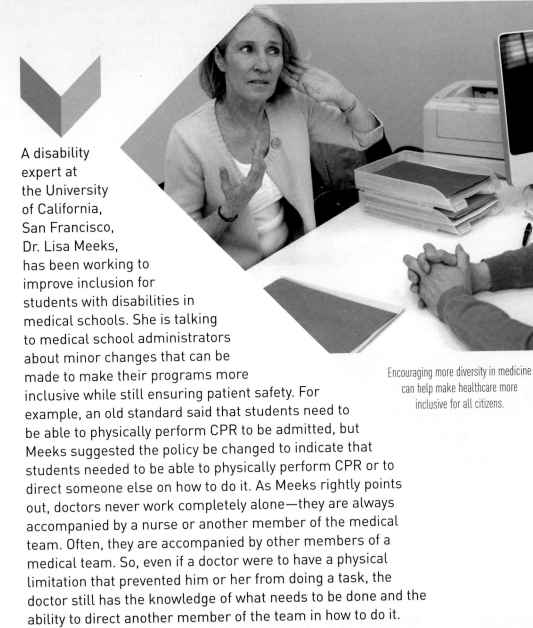

A disability
expert at
the University
of California,
San Francisco,
Dr. Lisa Meeks,
has been working to
improve inclusion for
students with disabilities in
medical schools. She is talking
to medical school administrators
about minor changes that can be
made to make their programs more
inclusive while still ensuring patient safety. For
example, an old standard said that students need to
be able to physically perform CPR to be admitted, but
Meeks suggested the policy be changed to indicate that
students needed to be able to physically perform CPR or to
direct someone else on how to do it. As Meeks rightly points
out, doctors never work completely alone—they are always
accompanied by a nurse or another member of the medical
team. Often, they are accompanied by other members of a
medical team. So, even if a doctor were to have a physical
limitation that prevented him or her from doing a task, the
doctor still has the knowledge of what needs to be done and the
ability to direct another member of the team in how to do it.

Encouraging more diversity in medicine
can help make healthcare more
inclusive for all citizens.

The hope is that by increasing the diversity in medical teams in
terms of the abilities of team members, healthcare will become
more accessible and effective for patients with disabilities. Not
only would the caregivers with disabilities have better insight
into the challenges faced by their patients with disabilities,
but their colleagues would learn from them about the unique
aspects of living with and working with people with disabilities.

Brian Skotko:

Raising Awareness and Helping Families

With the passage of laws such as the ADA and the IDEA (both passed in 1990), disability rights have come more into the public eye as civil rights, and the contributions of people with disabilities have become more widely recognized.

Working with Down Syndrome

One person who is working in the medical field both to bring awareness to developmental disabilities and to further medical knowledge in this area is Dr. Brian Skotko. Dr. Skotko's sister, Kristin, has Down syndrome, and he has devoted his career in the medical field to working with children with Down syndrome and other cognitive and developmental disabilities.

Dr. Brian Skotko is the director of the Down Syndrome Program at MGH.

A graduate of Duke University and Harvard Medical School, Dr. Skotko is the director of the Down Syndrome Program at Massachusetts General Hospital (MGH). He treats children with Down syndrome in his medical practice and is a leading clinical researcher in the field. He travels worldwide, sharing his research and knowledge about Down syndrome with other medical professionals.

Bringing Awareness

In addition to his thriving medical practice, though, Dr. Skotko has made it a point to enlighten people about the reality of life with a loved one with Down syndrome. For many years, there were misconceptions that having a child with Down syndrome would somehow be a burden to a family. Dr. Skotko, along with clinical social worker Sue Levine and Dr. Rick Goldstein, have

WHAT IS DOWN SYNDROME?

Down syndrome is a genetic condition that occurs in roughly 1 of 790 births. Currently, there are estimated to be around 210,000 people with Down syndrome living in the United States. In past decades, people with Down syndrome were either denied an education or were educated in segregated classrooms, where they often received life skills training but little other education. Now, more and more people with Down syndrome are being educated in inclusive classrooms among their typically developing peers, as well as participating in their communities.

studied families in the United States who have a member with Down syndrome. The results of studies showed overwhelmingly that families with a person with Down syndrome were happy. Parents and siblings of people with Down syndrome shared that they felt love and pride for their family members, and people with Down syndrome expressed that they lead happy and fulfilling lives. Research like this is helping to change society's and the medical community's view of people with developmental and cognitive disabilities like Down syndrome.

To further educate people about Down syndrome, Dr. Skotko has published books about Down syndrome aimed at nonmedical professionals, including *Fasten Your Seatbelt: A Crash Course on Down Syndrome for Brothers and Sisters*. In that book and related presentations, Dr. Skotko and coauthor Sue Levine outline the unique role that brothers and sisters of people with disabilities are in—as protectors, supporters, and also sometimes frustrated siblings.

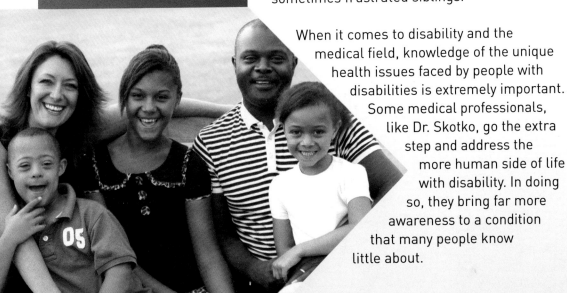

When it comes to disability and the medical field, knowledge of the unique health issues faced by people with disabilities is extremely important. Some medical professionals, like Dr. Skotko, go the extra step and address the more human side of life with disability. In doing so, they bring far more awareness to a condition that many people know little about.

A Progressive Field with Room to Grow

The United States is a melting pot of cultures, races, abilities, and socioeconomic classes. Encouraging diversity in the medical field will help make sure the healthcare needs of all citizens are met.

Medicine is a cooperative field. Doctors, nurses, technicians, and therapists all work together to provide patient care. For example, when a person is diagnosed with cancer, there is not just one doctor working on that person's care. There will be one or more oncologists, other specialists related to the area of the body affected by the cancer, many nurses, perhaps physical therapists if the cancer treatment resulted in a loss of ability to move or limitations in movement, and probably a counselor or therapist to help the patient deal with a difficult diagnosis. When there is diversity in the medical field, these teams of providers who work collaboratively on a person's care have the opportunity to learn from other providers' viewpoints and ideas.

Giving Back

A large problem in the United States is the lack of good healthcare for people living in poverty or other marginalized circumstances. Encouraging diversity helps address this problem, because medical professionals who grew up in

Diverse medical teams better represent the diversity of the US population, which leads to better medical care.

poor or marginalized circumstances are more likely to ultimately practice medicine in similar areas. They are also familiar with the struggles faced by their patients living in these circumstances. For example, people living in poverty often cannot afford very healthful foods for their families, which can then contribute to obesity or other health problems. Medical professionals who recognize these unique circumstances can often point patients to programs to help them gain access to more healthful foods, and they can counsel their patients on how to make healthy food choices on a limited budget.

Using Cultural Competence to Achieve Better Healthcare

Diversity in medicine is an advantage with regard to the increasing interest in eastern medicine. Some medical providers are now encouraging their patients to use techniques of eastern medicine in addition to following western medical practices. Such providers may offer access to acupuncture, meditation classes, tai chi, and more. It is a demonstration of cultural competence, but it is also a sign that practitioners of western medicine are beginning to realize that eastern and western philosophies can work together to improve a person's overall wellness.

As the population of the United States continues to grow in diversity, hopefully the medical field will follow suit.

Timeline

1849: Elizabeth Blackwell becomes the first woman to graduate from medical school in the United States.

1863: Mary Edwards Walker becomes the first female surgeon in the Civil War (and is thought to be the first female surgeon in general).

1864: Rebecca Lee Crumpler becomes the first black woman to earn a medical degree in the United States.

1866: Ann Preston becomes the first female dean of a US medical school.

1879: Mary Mahoney becomes the first black woman in the United States to complete nurse's training.

1889: Susan La Flesche Picotte becomes the first Native American woman to earn a medical degree in the United States.

1915: Bertha Van Hoosen becomes the first president and the cofounder of the American Medical Women's Association (AMWA).

1925: Mary Carson Breckinridge founds the Frontier Nursing Service, which still exists and provides healthcare to underserved, rural populations.

1947: Gerty Cori becomes the first woman from the United States to earn the Nobel Prize in Physiology or Medicine, for her discoveries about the catalytic conversion of glycogen.

1949: Helen Brooke Taussig establishes the specialty of pediatric cardiology with her publication of the book *Congenital Malformations of the Heart*. She later becomes the first female president of the American Heart Association (AHA).

1953: Virginia Apgar creates the Apgar score, a standardized tool for newborn evaluation that is still used today.

1969: Elisabeth Kübler-Ross publishes her book *On Death and Dying*, which has become a standard reference for healthcare professionals working with patients with terminal illness. The book established the five stages of the grieving process.

1974: Audrey Evans creates the Ronald McDonald House, a place for families to stay when children are receiving cancer treatment. There are now Ronald McDonald Houses all over the country, serving thousands of families yearly.

1981: Alexa Canady becomes the first black neurosurgeon in the United States.

1986: Patricia Bath creates a new device and approach to cataract surgery, called Laserphaco.

1990: Antonia Novello becomes the first woman and the first Hispanic to become US Surgeon General.

1993: Barbara Ross-Lee becomes the first black woman to become dean of a medical school.

1993: Joycelyn Elders is appointed the first black Surgeon General of the United States.

1998: Nancy Dickey becomes the first female president of the AMA.

2007: Emmett Chapelle, a black biochemist at the National Aeronautics and Space Administration (NASA), is inducted into the National Inventors Hall of Fame in 2007 in honor of his work on bioluminescence. His work led to advances in detecting the number of bacteria in water.

2007: Edna Adan Ismail, sometimes called the "Muslim Mother Teresa," is named to the Medical Mission Hall of Fame for her lifelong humanitarian work in the medical field.

2009: Black physician Regina Benjamin is named Surgeon General of the United States. Benjamin has received numerous awards and honors for her work in battling the obesity epidemic in the United States and working to promote better overall health.

2015: Bonnie Simpson Mason becomes the youngest person to receive the Diversity Award from the American Academy of Orthopaedic Surgeons (AAOS) for her work in making orthopedics more representative of and accessible to diverse patient populations. Simpson Mason founded a nonprofit organization that implements initiatives to try to diversify the medical workforce.

Glossary

acupuncture An eastern medical practice in which needles are inserted in the skin at specific points to treat physical, mental, and emotional conditions.

affinity A liking for something.

anecdotal Based on personal account, rather than fact or research.

cataract A medical condition that blurs the vision when the lens of the eye becomes progressively more opaque.

chiropractors People who practice chiropractic medicine, a method of manipulating the spine to address problems in various joints and body systems.

demographic A particular section of a population.

dialects Forms of a language that are particular to a specific region or social group.

electrocardiogram A display showing the electrical impulses in a person's heart.

ethnicity Belonging to a social group that has a common national or cultural tradition.

hypothyroidism Low activity of the thyroid gland, resulting in developmental delays.

impetigo A bacterial skin infection that is highly contagious.

Jim Crow Describes the practice of segregating black people from white people in the United States.

Latinx A gender-inclusive form of the word "Latino," often used by Latinos who are genderqueer.

linguistic Related to language.

marginalized Ignored or treated as insignificant.

median The midpoint value in a series of values, where an equal number of values fall above and below it.

neuropathology The study of diseases of the tissue in the nervous system.

occupational therapists Medical practitioners who work on everyday small-motor tasks that require specific coordination to perform.

ophthalmology The study and treatment of diseases and disorders of the eyes.

osteopath A doctor who treats medical issues by manipulating the bones, joints, and muscles.

physical therapists Medical practitioners who work on large-motor skills.

qi gong A Chinese medical treatment that involves physical exercises and breathing control.

Soviet Union A post-World War II group of communist countries overseen by the Russian government. The Soviet Union dissolved in 1991.

tai chi A Chinese system of exercise that uses sequences of very slow, controlled movements.

For Further Reading

Books

Currie-McGhee, Leanne K. *Careers in Medicine*. San Diego, CA: Referencepoint Press, 2017.

Hollar, Sherman. *Pioneers in Medicine: From the Classical World to Today*. New York, NY: Rosen Publishing, 2012.

Latta, Susan M. *Bold Women of Medicine: 21 Stories of Astounding Discoveries, Daring Surgeries, and Healing Breakthroughs*. Chicago, IL: Chicago Review Press, 2017.

Thomson, Betsy. *Meditation, My Friend: Meditation for Kids and Beginners of All Ages*. Quakertown, PA: Betsy Thomson Publishing, 2013.

Websites

BAM! Body and Mind
www.cdc.gov/bam
This site hosted by the Centers for Disease Control is a great place to learn more about health, nutrition, physical activity, and safety.

FDA For Kids
www.fda.gov/ForConsumers/ByAudience/ForKids
This site by the U.S. Food & Drug Administration allows children to learn about health and safety through songs, quizzes, interactive games, and crossword puzzles.

KidsHealth
https://kidshealth.org/en/kids
This site has numerous pages to help young people learn more about the body, health, medical terms, puberty, and more. It is available in English and Spanish.

MedlinePlus
https://medlineplus.gov/childrenspage.html
This page by the U.S. National Library of Medicine allows young people to learn more about health topics and play games based on the topic.

Index